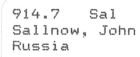

RUSSIA

ARCTIC
OCEAN

BARENTS
SEA

KARA
SEA

NORWAY
DEN.
SWEDEN
FINLAND
BALTIC SEA
ESTONIA
LATVIA
LITHUANIA
St. Petersburg
KARELIA
Arkhangel'sk
YAMAL PENINSULA

KALININGRAD
OBLAST

POLAND

BELARUS

MOSCOW

Usinsk

KOMI

RUSSIAN

MOLDOVA

UKRAINE

Kursk

Nizhniy Novgorod

MARI

UDMURTIA

Naberezhniye Chelny

Yekaterinburg

MORDOVIA

TATARSTAN

CHUVASHIA

Tol'yatti

Samara

BASHKORTOSTAN

Chelyabinsk

Magnitogorsk

Omsk

Novosibirsk

Novokuznets

BLACK
SEA

KARACHAEVO-
CHERKESSIA

Volgograd

KALMYKIA

ADYGEYA

Stavropol

CHECHNYA

KABARDINO-
BALKARIA

NORTH
OSSETI

INGUSHETIYA

GEORGIA

DAGESTAN

CASPIAN SEA

KAZAKHSTAN

GORN
ALTA

ARMENIA

AZERBAIJAN

TURKEY

IRAN

TURKMENISTAN

UZBEKISTAN

KYRGYZSTAN

0   500 miles
0   1,000 km

RUSSIA

John Sallnow
and Tatyana Saiko

RAINTREE
STECK-VAUGHN
PUBLISHERS
The Steck-Vaughn Company

Austin, Texas

Published by Raintree Steck-Vaughn Publishers, an imprint of
Steck-Vaughn Company

Design and typesetting Roger Kohn Designs
Editors Diana Russell, Pam Wells
Picture research Valerie Mulcahy
Illustration János Márffy
Commissioning editor Debbie Fox

We are grateful to the following for permission
to reproduce photographs:
Front Cover: Tatyana Saiko *above,*
SCR Photo Library/David Toase *below;*
B & C Alexander, pages 17 *above,* 37 *above;* Ardea London
Ltd, pages 39 *below* (J M Labat), 41 (Ferrero/Labat); The
Associated Press Ltd, page 13 (Misha Japaridze); Colorific!,
page 15 (Bob Krist/Black Star); The Environmental Picture
Library, pages 11 (Pierre Gleizes), 39 *above* (Mark Warford);
JVZ, page 19 (Eugene Poggeo); Novosti (London), pages 12
above, 16, 26 *above* (Dmitri Donskoy), 26 *below,* 30/31, 33;
Rex Features Ltd, page 43 *below* (R Roderni White); SCR
Photo Library, pages 23 and 43 *above* (David Toase); Tatyana
Saiko, pages 34, 42; Frank Spooner Pictures/GAMMA, pages
27 *below* (A Hernandez/Liaison), 29 (Hires-Merillon), 35
(Swersey/Liaison); Tony Stone Images, pages 8/9 and 24
above (Gavin Hellier); Sygma, pages 14 and 20 (Jacques
Langevin), 24 *below* (Epix), 28 (Sparonenkov), 30
(J P Laffont); Sygma Paris, page 32; Travel Ink, pages 12
below and 18/19 (David Toase), 25 (Life File/Oleg
Svyatoslavsky); TRIP, pages 17 *below* (V Larionov), 21 (Bob
Turner), 22 *above* (F Torrance), 22 *below* (M Kenkin), 27
above (V Kanashev), 36 (A Kuznetsov), 37 *below* (Bob
Turner); Zefa, pages 8 (G Steemans), 18, 38 (Dr Hans
Kramarz); Viktor Zhivotchenko, page 10/11.

The statistics given in this book are the most up to date
available at the time of going to press

Printed in Hong Kong by Wing King Tong

1 2 3 4 5 6 7 8 9 0 HK 99 98 97 96

Library of Congress Cataloging-in-Publication Data
Sallnow, John.
Russia / John Sallnow and Tatyana Saiko.
p. cm. – (Country fact files)
Includes bibliographical references and index.
ISBN 0-8172-4625-8
1. Russia (Federation) – Juvenile literature. 2. Russia
(Federation) I. Saiko, Tatyana. II. Title. III. Series.
DK510.23.S25 1997
947–dc20
96-32783
CIP AC

Special thanks to the children of School No. 599,
Tushinskiy District, North West Region, Moscow,
who are pictured on the front cover.

CONTENTS

Words that are explained in the glossary are printed in
SMALL CAPITALS the first time they are mentioned in the text.

INTRODUCTION

The Russian Federation is the largest country in the world and has the sixth biggest population. It is so vast that it would almost be possible to fit the territory of the United States into the Federation twice. The country straddles the two continents of Europe and Asia, stretching from the Baltic Sea to the shores of the Pacific Ocean.

The Federation is also known as "Russia," a term that comes from the ancient name of "Rus." For centuries, Russia was ruled by the TSARS, until they were overthrown in the Russian Revolution of 1917. This was followed by a period of civil war. From 1922 to 1991, Russia was part of the Soviet Union, which was a banding together of 15 republics that were usually known as Soviet Socialist Republics. For this reason, the Soviet Union was also called the Union of Soviet Socialist Republics (USSR).

For many years, the Soviet Union and the United States were rival "superpowers," and there was strong competition between them. However, today the USSR no longer exists,

▲ *This extended family (including uncles, aunts, grandparents, cousins) lives in traditionally decorated wooden houses in a village in southern Siberia. Living conditions here can be poor. For example, village roads are often not paved, but just consist of bare earth, and houses may not have running water.*

and respect and cooperation have replaced rivalry. Russia has taken the former Soviet Union's seat at world organizations such as the United Nations, and it still has much influence in world political affairs.

Since 1991, the country has undergone rapid and dramatic changes, which have affected all aspects of life there. In this book, you can find out what Russia is like today. You will read about the country's varied landscape and climate, its wealth of natural resources, the makeup of its

▼ **Trinity and St. Sergius, Russia's largest monastery, was built in the Moscow region in the 16th century. Today it is the chief center of the Russian Orthodox Church.**

RUSSIA AT A GLANCE

● Area: 6,592,812 square miles (17,075,400 sq km)
● Population (1995 estimate): 148,000,000
● Population density (1995): 22.5 people per sq mile (9 per sq km)
● Capital: Moscow (called Moskva in Russian), population 8,793,000
● Other main cities: St. Petersburg 4.9 million; Novosibirsk 1.4 million
● Highest mountain: Mount Elbrus, 18,510 feet (5,642 m)
● Longest river: Lena, 2,734 miles (4,400 km)
● Language: Russian
● Major religion: Russian Orthodox (Islam in some republics)
● Life expectancy (1994): 57 years for men; 71 years for women
● Currency: Ruble, written as R
● Economy: Rapid move to market economy and PRIVATIZATION since January 1992
● Major resources: Oil, natural gas, coal, iron ore, copper, gold, nickel, silver, tungsten, diamonds, uranium (but much lies below the PERMAFROST)
● Major products: Aircraft, trucks, cars, tractors, combine harvesters, scientific goods, cameras, wood, wood products, wooden dolls, caviar, vodka
● Environmental problems: Still suffering effects of world's worst nuclear accident in 1986 at Chernobyl (now in independent Ukraine), pollution of waterways, rivers, and lakes by oil seepage, careless use of chemical fertilizers in agriculture

population, how people go about their daily lives, and how the country is governed. You will also read about the country's agriculture, trade, and industry, its transportation facilities, its environmental advantages and problems, and the prospect for Russia's future in the twenty-first century.

Russia can be divided into several physical regions. The European part runs from the Baltic Sea in the west to the Ural mountains in the east, while the south includes the mountainous slopes of the north Caucasus. The Arctic islands and coasts have cold, polar "deserts" and a treeless landscape known as TUNDRA. To the south, this is replaced by vast coniferous forests called TAIGA, which cover large areas in Europe, central Siberia, and the Far East. The southern part of the European plain and west Siberia have open grasslands known as STEPPES. The great size of the country means that vast belts or zones of vegetation continue for hundreds and thousands of miles.

In the northern European area, there is dense coniferous forest, which turns into mixed and deciduous forest to the south. The steppes have a very rich soil, called CHERNOZEM, or "black earth," because of its color. The Caucasus mountain range varies in height between 2,625 feet (800 m) and over 16,000 feet (5,000 m). It lies between the Black Sea and the Caspian Sea and forms the southern border of European Russia. In these southern regions, there are areas of semidesert, and even a desert in Kalmykia.

The Urals are less rugged than the Caucasus, with an average height of around 3,300 feet (1,000 m). There are several natural passes between

◀ *At 15,585 ft (4,750 m), Klyuchevskaya Sopka is Eurasia's highest active volcano. Located in Russia's Kamchatka Peninsula, it has erupted 10 times since 1945, most recently in 1991.*

the mountains. The highest peak in the Urals is Mount Narodnaya in the north, at 6,217 feet (1,895 m). The range forms the boundary between the two continents of Europe and Asia, so that Russia is one-quarter in Europe but three-quarters in Asia.

To the east of the Urals lie Siberia and the Far East. The western part of Siberia is a huge lowland which stretches 992 miles (1,600 km) across and 1,488 miles (2,400 km) from north to south, making it the largest plain in the world. It is a vast frozen area in winter and a gigantic marshland in summer. It also contains large deposits of oil and natural gas.

East Siberia and the Far East contain several mountain ranges, in between which

KEY FACTS

● Russia's Volga River is the longest river in Europe (2,293 miles or 3,690 km).

● Russia measures 5,592 miles (9,000 km) from east to west, and 2,480 miles (4,000 km) from north to south.

● The country covers 11 time zones. Before people in Moscow have sat down to lunch, those in eastern Siberia have already gone to bed.

● Russia's largest lake is Lake Baykal in Siberia, covering 12,162 square miles (31,500 sq km) and containing one-fifth of the world's freshwater resources.

▼ *The European taiga is part of a massive zone of coniferous forest. This is Pechora National Park in Komi Republic.*

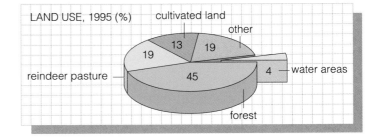

LAND USE, 1995 (%)
cultivated land 13
other 19
reindeer pasture 19
forest 45
water areas 4

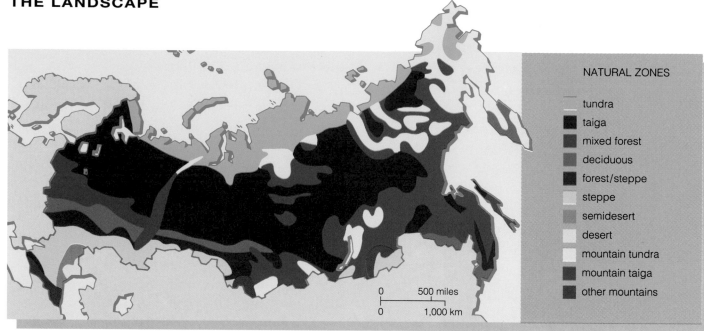

NATURAL ZONES

- tundra
- taiga
- mixed forest
- deciduous
- forest/steppe
- steppe
- semidesert
- desert
- mountain tundra
- mountain taiga
- other mountains

0   500 miles

0   1,000 km

flow some of the longest rivers in the world, such as the Lena (2,734 miles or 4,400 km), the Irtysh (2,634 miles or 4,248 km), and the Yenisey (2,543 miles or 4,102 km). The natural vegetation here is the taiga forest, consisting of larch, spruce, and pine, below which lies the permafrost. This is permanently frozen ground that can be up to 2,625 feet (800 m) thick. Only the upper 8–60 inches (20–150 cm) thaw out during the summer. Most of the permafrost has not thawed out since the last Ice Age. Bones of woolly mammoths are often found here — and sometimes even a whole baby mammoth.

▼ *Baykal, the world's deepest lake at 5,316 feet (1,637 m). This rock on the shore of the lake is called "Two Brothers."*

◄ *Russians call Europe's longest river "Mother Volga." It has been a key transportation route for 1,000 years. This is its junction with the Oka River, near Nizhniy Novgorod.*

CLIMATE AND WEATHER

▲ *Encouraged by "Father Frost," a young "walrus" braves New Year temperatures of 5°F (–15°C) for the air and 33–36°F (1–2°C) for the water.*

Since Russia is such a large country, there are major variations in its climate. But generally it has long, cold winters and warm or hot summers. This climate is very similar to parts of the United States. In January, most of Russia has temperatures below zero, and there is a "pole of cold" in northeastern Siberia. The coldest city on Earth is Verkhoyansk. Near here the world's lowest temperature (apart from Antarctica) was recorded at –96°F (–71°C). In Siberia and the Far East, when the temperature falls to –40°F (–40°C), children do not have to go to school. In the European part of Russia, including Moscow, it does not get as cold as this, so here children are excused from school when the temperature reaches –22°F (–30°C). Only on the Black Sea coast are January temperatures in the cities above the freezing point.

In July, all of Russia has warm or hot temperatures — up to 95°F (35°C) at the "winter pole of cold" at Verkhoyansk. This city has the greatest temperature range of anywhere in the world — more than 110°F.

Russians love to sunbathe and swim even in winter. River ice is removed and people swim in the cold water. They are known as "walrus." Many believe their icy swim helps to prevent them from becoming ill in the long Russian winter.

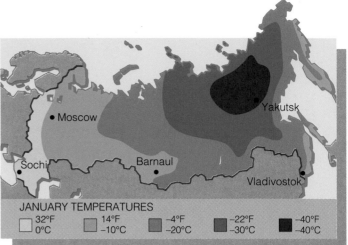

JANUARY TEMPERATURES

| | 32°F
0°C | | 14°F
–10°C | | –4°F
–20°C | | –22°F
–30°C | | –40°F
–40°C |

KEY FACTS

● 16% of Russia's territory lies inside the Arctic Circle.

● Average temperatures in Russia range from 30°F to –58°F (–1° to –50°C) in January, and from 34°F to –77°F (1° to 25°C) in July.

● Average January temperatures in Vladivostok are 20°F less than in Nice (France), although both cities are on the same latitude.

● Siberia has an average 15.6–19.5 inches of snow a year, while the Arctic north of European Russia has an average of 27.3–31.2 inches.

● Although the Black Sea coast is still popular with Russian vacationers, rising prices mean that it is sometimes cheaper for them to vacation in Cyprus instead.

▲ **North of the Arctic Circle, the ocean and rivers are frozen for more than six months of the year. Ships can easily become trapped in ice here.**

Yakutsk

Moscow

Barnaul

JULY TEMPERATURES

☐ 50°F 10°C	☐ 59°F 15°C	▨ 68°F 20°C	▤ 77°F 25°C	■ 86°F 30°C

▶ *Many people spend sunny weekends at city beaches. These sunbathers are relaxing on Peter and Paul Island at the mouth of the Neva, St. Petersburg.*

In Siberia, summer is short and winter returns quickly at the beginning of September. But in European Russia there is more gradual change during September and October. Moscow's first snow normally comes in November, and then five months of winter begin. In the northern parts of Siberia, winter lasts for up to nine months.

At Yakutsk in the Russian Far East, temperatures are below freezing for seven months of the year, compared to six months at Barnaul in east Siberia, and four and a half months in Moscow. The same period of freezing temperatures is found at Vladivostok on the Pacific Ocean. The city of Sochi on the Black Sea has daytime temperatures above freezing all year. Its annual rainfall distribution reflects its Mediterranean-type climate.

Moscow and Barnaul have the greatest rainfall in summer, especially in July. In Vladivostok the greatest rainfall comes in August and September, sometimes with tropical cyclones and typhoons from the Sea of Japan. Total annual rain and snowfall here can reach 40 inches (1,000 mm). In contrast, Yakutsk has relatively little rain or snow. In the steppe and semidesert zones, there is little moisture all year round. Areas around the Caspian Sea may have less than 6 inches (150 mm) of rain a year. Droughts and hot winds are common.

This great range in climate and weather means that Russian people have to adapt their lives accordingly. For instance, in the winter they take advantage of powerful central heating systems at home and dress in furs when they go outside.

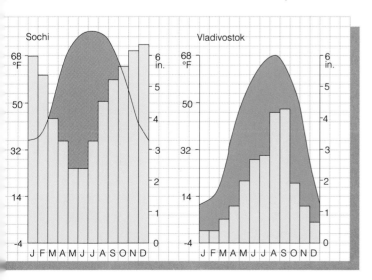

NATURAL RESOURCES

Russia has a vast wealth of natural resources, with deposits of every known useful mineral. It is the world's largest producer of natural gas and nickel and is the third largest producer of oil and coal. It is also the world's second largest producer of diamonds, after Australia, with 1994 production of 17 million carats. And it is the world's largest producer of asbestos, with 880,000 tons mined in 1994.

Many of the minerals are found in Siberia and the Far East, where approximately 63 percent of territory lies under the permafrost. Powerful steam hoses are used to melt it, which adds to the cost of extracting the mineral ores. Iron ore is found in the Kursk region and aluminum ores in the north of European Russia. For centuries, the Ural Mountains have been exploited for their rich resources of copper, iron, molybdenum, chromium, and precious stones. This is still an important mining and industrial center.

In the mid-1980s, Russia was the world's largest producer of iron and steel. Today, it is the third largest producer of pig, or crude,

KEY FACTS

● Russia's total coal reserves are estimated at more than 5,500 billion tons, of which 3,850 billion tons are in the Tunguska-Lena basin.
● Much of Russia's oil and natural gas is exported to Western Europe and is used to pay for food imports.
● Russia has the largest reserves of coniferous forest in the world – 84.7 billion cubic yards (64.8 billion cubic meters).
● In 1993, 12 percent of total electric energy was generated by nuclear power.
● Russia has reserves of about 176 billion tons of peat, or 60 percent of the world's total – mainly located in west Siberia.

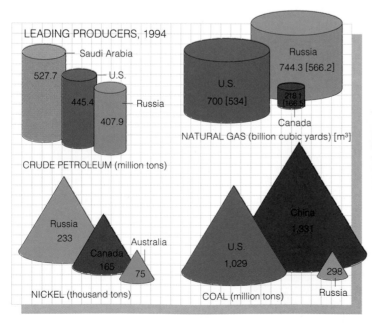

LEADING PRODUCERS, 1994

CRUDE PETROLEUM (million tons)
Saudi Arabia 527.7
U.S. 445.4
Russia 407.9

NATURAL GAS (billion cubic yards) [m³]
Russia 744.3 [566.2]
U.S. 700 [534]
Canada 218.1 [166.5]

NICKEL (thousand tons)
Russia 233
Canada 165
Australia 75

COAL (million tons)
China 1,331
U.S. 1,029
Russia 298

▲ The Mirniy diamond mine in Sakha Republic. Diamonds are extracted from each level by strip mining.

iron, at 45 million tons in 1994, after China and the United States. Russia also occupied fourth place in the production of steel ingots in 1994, with 53.7 million tons, after Japan, China, and the U.S.

Gold is found in Siberia, and in 1994, Russia was fourth in world production of it, with 324,076 pounds (147,000 kg), after South Africa, the U.S., and Australia.

Many valuable ores and minerals are located in the remote parts of Siberia and the Far East. Higher wages have to be paid to encourage people to work in these harsh environments – up to three times the average wages for similar jobs in Moscow. But major oil and gas spills have caused considerable environmental damage. Many wetland areas in Siberia are contaminated with crude oil.

▲ **High-pressure steam hoses are used to melt the permafrost that lies over gas deposits in the Yamal Peninsula.**

▶ **The taiga has rich timber resources. Massive rafts made of logs are sent down rivers or across lakes to sawmills.**

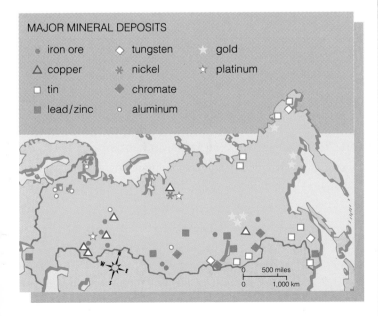

MAJOR MINERAL DEPOSITS

- iron ore
- ◇ tungsten
- ★ gold
- △ copper
- ✳ nickel
- ☆ platinum
- □ tin
- ◆ chromate
- ▪ lead/zinc
- ○ aluminum

0 — 500 miles
0 — 1,000 km

POPULATION

NATIONALITIES

The last full census in Russia in 1989 listed 129 nationalities living in the territory. The Russians are the largest national grouping, with an estimated total population of 122 million in 1995. They belong to the European grouping known as the Slavs. Other Slav peoples living in Russia include Ukrainians and Belorussians. Over the years, members of all these groups have migrated to areas of Asiatic Russia, too. In 1989, according to the census, the population of Russia's northern regions stood at 199,000, divided into 29 nationalities. These groups are all very small. None of them is even 0.1 percent

◄*The Yakuts are the second largest native grouping in Siberia. They live in the coldest part of the region, and celebrate their summer festival by dancing, singing, and eating feasts.*

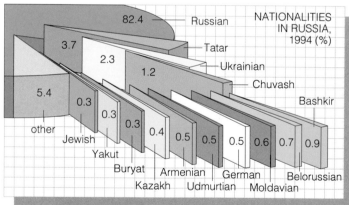

NATIONALITIES IN RUSSIA, 1994 (%)

82.4	Russian
3.7	Tatar
2.3	Ukrainian
1.2	Chuvash
	Bashkir
5.4	
other	
0.3 Jewish	
0.3 Yakut	
0.3 Buryat	
0.4 Kazakh	
0.5 Armenian	
0.5 Udmurtian	
0.5 German	
0.6 Moldavian	
0.7	
0.9 Belorussian	

of Russia's total population. The largest group is the Nentsy, with 34,000 members, while the smallest are the Entsi and the Oroki, with only about 200 each.

The lifestyles of people in Siberia and the Far East can be very different from those in European Russia, because of the cold weather and the harsh environment.

◀ ▼ *In the cities, most Russians live in tall apartment buildings. Since housing can be scarce, the apartments are small compared to those in the U.S. One room is often used as both a living room and a bedroom.*

KEY FACTS

● 30 million Russians have migrated to Siberia since the first settlers arrived in the 17th century.

● In 1994, the number of refugees and migrants in Russia increased from 447,933 to 702,451.

● Between January 1992 and January 1994, the population of Siberia fell by 89,000 and that of the Far East by 244,000.

● In 1994, there were 34 million women workers in Russia, 49% of the workforce.

● In 1994, 21 million senior citizens were women, almost three times the number of male senior citizens.

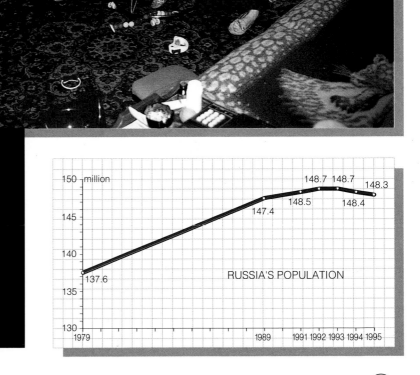

RUSSIA'S POPULATION

150 ┬million
148.7 148.7 148.3
148.5 148.4
147.4
145
140
137.6
135
130
1979   1989   1991 1992 1993 1994 1995

► **People in the Arctic areas must dress warmly, because of the extreme cold. These Nentsy children wear gloves, boots, and hoods made of reindeer fur to protect themselves from the freezing winds.**

1,210		China
913		India
261		U.S.
191		Indonesia
160		Brazil
148		Russia

POPULATIONS OF THE WORLD'S LARGEST COUNTRIES, 1994 (millions)

People such as the Yakuts of Siberia refer to those in Moscow as if they live in a totally different country.

THE CITIES

After World War II, as a result of rapid industrialization, many people moved from the countryside to the cities. The proportion of Russia's population living in towns and cities rose from 34 percent in 1945 to 52 percent in 1959 and 73 percent in 1994. This involved the migration of 40 million people, all in need of a place to live. The result was the building of huge blocks of apartments in every major city in the country.

However, recently there has been a shift in the opposite direction. Between 1991 and 1995, Russia's urban population fell by 1.5 million, while the rural population increased by 1.3 million. One reason for this change

is the high cost of living in Russian cities today. Many food prices are similar to those in the United States, while in 1996 the wages of most working people were around 10 percent or less of the average wages in the U.S.

POPULATION LEVELS

Not only is the proportion of city dwellers declining, but Russia's overall population is falling, too. The total number of people in the country fell by 300,000 in 1993 and by another 100,000 in 1994. The birthrate in 1994 stood at 9.6 per 1,000 people, down from 12.1 per 1,000 in 1991. The typical

Russian family today has one or two children. The government encourages large families by presenting mothers with a medal to honor their contribution to society if a family has five or more children.

The low birthrate is partly because of the cost of raising a family, even though the majority of Russian women work full-time. Although things are changing, generally women are expected to do all the housework and work outside the home. This is why most women find it easier to have smaller families.

THE COUNTRYSIDE

People living in the villages still have very few services, besides radio and television. Many have to go to the village well to draw water for their everyday needs. A family normally keeps its own cow to supply milk and chickens to provide eggs. People also grow their own fruits, such as apples and cherries, and vegetables, such as potatoes and onions.

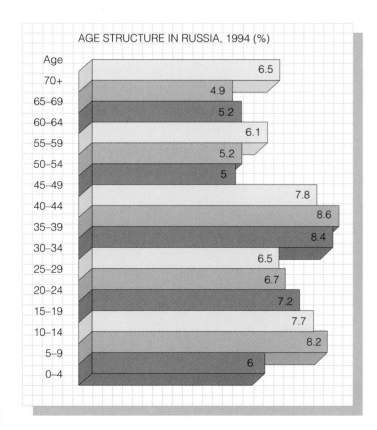

AGE STRUCTURE IN RUSSIA, 1994 (%)

Age	%
70+	6.5
65–69	4.9
60–64	5.2
55–59	6.1
50–54	5.2
45–49	5
40–44	7.8
35–39	8.6
30–34	8.4
25–29	6.5
20–24	6.7
15–19	7.2
10–14	7.7
5–9	8.2
0–4	6

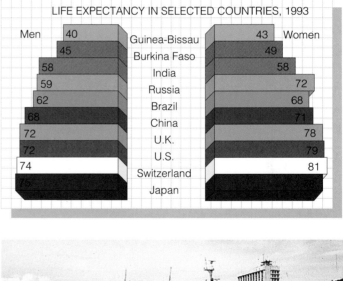

LIFE EXPECTANCY IN SELECTED COUNTRIES, 1993

Men	Country	Women
40	Guinea-Bissau	43
45	Burkina Faso	49
58	India	58
59	Russia	72
62	Brazil	68
68	China	71
72	U.K.	78
72	U.S.	79
74	Switzerland	81
75	Japan	

► *Because of population movements, many Russians of European descent now live in Siberia and the Far East – like those pictured here, in Vladivostok.*

RELIGION

In the time of the USSR, schoolchildren were told that God did not exist. However, today many people in Russia do believe in God, and most of these belong to the Russian Orthodox Church. It has strict rules and rituals. For instance, it requires people to stand during the sermons that can sometimes be quite long. Islam is the main religion in the southern republics of European Russia. Protestants and Buddhists are common in the Asiatic part of the country. Other religions include Catholicism and Judaism, but many Jewish people have moved to Israel since the late 1980s.

EDUCATION

Children start primary school at the age of 6 or 7 and leave at 10 or 11. Education is compulsory up to the age of 16, but many stay on until they are 18, when they may take entrance examinations for a

FESTIVALS AND HOLIDAYS

January 1–2	NEW YEAR HOLIDAY
January 7	RUSSIAN ORTHODOX CHRISTMAS
February 23	RUSSIAN ARMY DAY
March 8	INTERNATIONAL WOMEN'S DAY
April 2	DAY OF THE UNITY OF THE PEOPLE
May 1–2	FIRST OF MAY DAY and WORKERS' SOLIDARITY DAY
May 9	VICTORY DAY
June 12	INDEPENDENCE DAY
November 7	RUSSIAN REVOLUTION HOLIDAY

▶ *A traditional wooden house, or "dacha," in the countryside. Here city dwellers grow fruit trees, vegetables, and potatoes. Homegrown produce provides an important source of food for the winter.*

◀ *Drinking tea from a huge teapot, or "samovar." Once heated by hot coals inside them, most samovars today are electrically heated.*

university or institute of higher education. At the age of 16, other students can go on to professional and technical schools. There they learn special technical skills in order to enter a profession.

Some schools are now privately run, while others provide teaching in the language of one of Russia's many national groupings. There are also special language schools where several subjects are taught in one foreign language. In those schools children also study the literature of the country concerned. The first "special English schools" opened in Moscow in the mid-1950s.

The school year runs from September 1 to the end of May or beginning of June, so Russian schoolchildren have long summer vacations. There are also three brief breaks in autumn, spring, and the New Year.

KEY FACTS

● In 1992, 40 different religious denominations were registered in Russia.
● Most Russian schools teach English as a foreign language.
● In September 1994, 2.5 million students were enrolled in 553 higher education institutes and universities.
● In 1993, there were 12,600 hospitals and clinics, and 1 doctor for every 222 people (compared with 1 for every 444 people in the United States).
● Every Russian citizen has to have an annual medical checkup.
● Children under 14 years old are not allowed to work.
● The standard work week is 40 hours long.
● Until the late 1980s, advertisements were not shown on Russian television.

▶ *Construction of the Moscow underground railroad (metro) began in 1935. It now has 153 stations, connecting remote residential areas with the city center. The Arbat metro station, shown here, is one of the oldest and most beautiful.*

▲ *There are many contrasts in modern Russia. This elderly woman is begging outside one of Moscow's most expensive stores.*

HEALTH

The health care system in Russia is free for everyone and includes the medical service of clinics and hospitals in each district of a city or rural area. Most schools also have a doctor or nurse. Medical aid is more difficult to obtain in the Arctic regions and in the remote areas of Siberia and the Far East. Helicopters are used to bring health professionals to these regions.

SPORTS AND LEISURE

Sports are an everyday part of Russian life. They are compulsory at schools. Children train in the school gymnasiums, outdoors, and in the nearest swimming pools. Winter sports are popular in Russia, and it is common for families to go skating or skiing on weekends. Hockey and figure skating

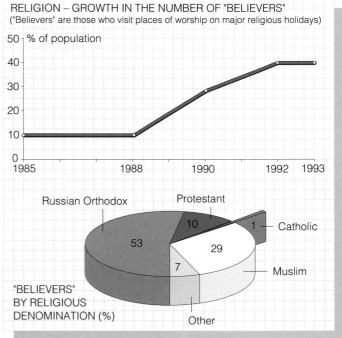

RELIGION – GROWTH IN THE NUMBER OF "BELIEVERS"
("Believers" are those who visit places of worship on major religious holidays)

% of population

| 1985 | 1988 | 1990 | 1992 | 1993 |

"BELIEVERS" BY RELIGIOUS DENOMINATION (%)

- Russian Orthodox 53
- Protestant 10
- Catholic 1
- Muslim 29
- Other 7

◀ *The Moscow* PATRIARCH, *Alexei II, became head of the Russian Orthodox Church in 1988, when the church celebrated 1,000 years of Christianity in Russia.*

are enjoyed by many, and Russia's hockey team and figure skaters are among the world's leaders. In summer, children often go to summer camps where they play all kinds of sports and enjoy leisure activities for a month or two. Football, volleyball, and basketball are among the most popular summer sports.

Many Russians have a summer house, or "dacha," in the countryside where they spend weekends or summer vacations and where they grow fruits and vegetables.

Russian people like to celebrate holidays. They are very hospitable, inviting many guests home and treating them to lots of food. Birthdays are the favorite holidays, with New Year holidays not far behind. The most important person at New Year is Father Frost (similar to Santa Claus), who

is accompanied by his assistant, the Snowgirl. Russian Christmas is celebrated 13 days later than in the United States, because the Russian Orthodox Church follows a calendar in use in previous centuries. And because 30 million Russians died in World War II, Victory Day, held on May 9, is also an important date.

In recent years there have been many changes in the lives of Russian people. Some have become very rich, but others have become poor as prices for many goods have increased.

▼ *The school year starts on September 1, when celebrations are held in schools and children bring flowers for their teachers.*

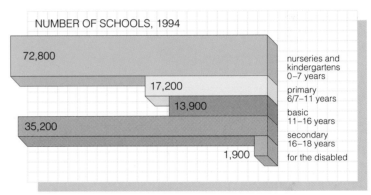

NUMBER OF SCHOOLS, 1994

72,800	nurseries and kindergartens 0–7 years
17,200	primary 6/7–11 years
13,900	basic 11–16 years
35,200	secondary 16–18 years
1,900	for the disabled

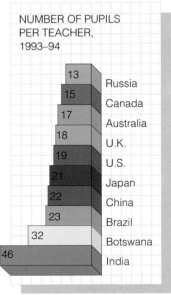

NUMBER OF PUPILS PER TEACHER, 1993–94

13	Russia
15	Canada
17	Australia
18	U.K.
19	U.S.
21	Japan
22	China
23	Brazil
32	Botswana
46	India

■ RULES AND LAWS

◀ Britain's Queen Elizabeth II made her first visit to Russia in October 1994. She is shown here with President Boris Yeltsin and the Mayor of Moscow, Yuri Luzhkov.

▶ "Omon" is a special police force dealing with terrorism and criminal gangs. This Omon unit is holding a training exercise aimed at arresting a "suspect."

After the end of COMMUNISM in 1991, Russia established a Federal Assembly that consists of two chambers. The upper chamber is called the Federation Council and has 178 nominated members. They do not serve for a fixed term, but continue for as long as they are reelected as leaders in the regions. The lower chamber is called the State Duma and consists of 450 members; half are elected from party lists, while the other half are elected by the regions. The most powerful political figure is the president.

The Russian president is the head of state and commander of the armed forces. He or she is similar to the President of the United States. The president can issue decrees on many subjects, such as defense, foreign policy, and financial matters.

The Russian government and the seat of power are located in the capital, Moscow.

◀ The Russian emblem shows the two-headed eagle of the tsars and an image of the patron saint, St. George.

▼ The Russian flag.

KEY FACTS

● In June 1991, Boris Yeltsin was elected as the first president of the Russian Federation.
● In December 1995, elections were held for the State Duma. The Russian Communist Party gained the largest number of seats.
● In January 1996, Russia joined the Council of Europe.
● In June 1996, Boris Yeltsin ran for president again. This time he did not win enough votes. In the runoff held in early July, Yeltsin won.
● In 1996, the Russian army consisted of 1.5 million soldiers. Almost all the ordinary soldiers are drafted and serve for a minimum of 2 years.

The president's office is in the Kremlin.

In each of Russia's 89 regions there is a presidential representative, a system that allows the president to stay in touch with the regions and keep informed about political issues.

The legal system reflects the great diversity of Russia's peoples, since each republic and region has its own court. The highest court is the Constitutional Court of the Federation, located in Moscow.

The police forces of Russia are divided into three main groups. There are the frontier guards, who control entry to and exit from the country and protect the state's borders; the traffic police, who control roads both inside cities and between towns and cities; and the militia, who patrol the streets and deal with general issues relating to law and order and the civilian population.

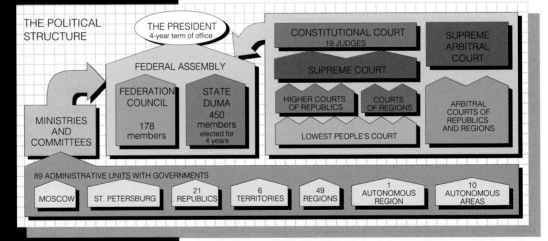

THE POLITICAL STRUCTURE

THE PRESIDENT
4-year term of office

FEDERAL ASSEMBLY

FEDERATION COUNCIL
178 members

STATE DUMA
450 members elected for 4 years

MINISTRIES AND COMMITTEES

CONSTITUTIONAL COURT
19 JUDGES

SUPREME ARBITRAL COURT

SUPREME COURT

HIGHER COURTS OF REPUBLICS

COURTS OF REGIONS

ARBITRAL COURTS OF REPUBLICS AND REGIONS

LOWEST PEOPLE'S COURT

89 ADMINISTRATIVE UNITS WITH GOVERNMENTS

MOSCOW | ST. PETERSBURG | 21 REPUBLICS | 6 TERRITORIES | 49 REGIONS | 1 AUTONOMOUS REGION | 10 AUTONOMOUS AREAS

▶ *Women in the Chechnya Republic protesting against the war there, which began in December 1994. The poster shows Chechen President Dudaev, who was killed in April 1996.*

FOOD AND FARMING

Farming in Russia highlights the varied pattern of land use, due to the great differences in the country's climatic regions. Most of Russia's cultivated area forms a large triangular shape, with its base on the western border and the highest point at Irkutsk in eastern Siberia. To the north of this area it is generally too cold to grow crops in the fields, although it is possible to cultivate crops in greenhouses. Because of the harsh climate and the long Russian winters, the cereal crops that do well are those that are known to be the most hardy. Russia is the world's leading producer of barley, oats, and potatoes; but it is only the

▲ **Harvesting beets near Moscow. Agriculture in this region is primarily aimed at meeting the demands of its huge urban population.**

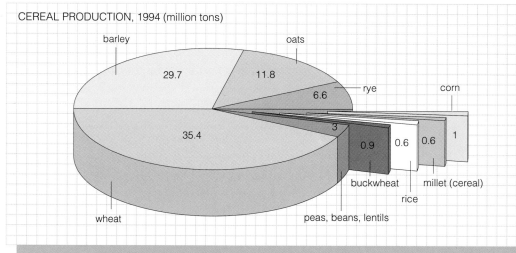

CEREAL PRODUCTION, 1994 (million tons)

- barley 29.7
- oats 11.8
- rye 6.6
- corn 1
- wheat 35.4
- 3
- buckwheat 0.9
- rice 0.6
- millet (cereal) 0.6
- peas, beans, lentils

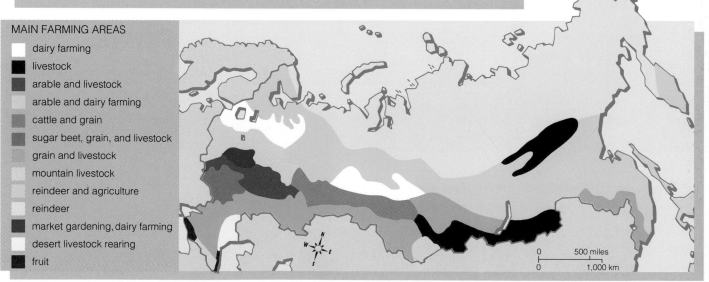

MAIN FARMING AREAS

- dairy farming
- livestock
- arable and livestock
- arable and dairy farming
- cattle and grain
- sugar beet, grain, and livestock
- grain and livestock
- mountain livestock
- reindeer and agriculture
- reindeer
- market gardening, dairy farming
- desert livestock rearing
- fruit

0   500 miles
0   1,000 km

KEY FACTS

● In 1994, Russia had 29.4 million head of cattle, 17.6 million sheep, and 14.5 million pigs.

● Food imports to Russia grew by 40% during 1995.

● Bread consumption by the average Russian is three times that of the average American.

● When the first McDonald's Restaurant opened in Moscow in 1990, lines of 5,000 people formed outside. The cost of a burger and fries was equal to half an average day's wages.

● People who live in the Arctic north and Siberia often eat reindeer meat as part of their diet.

● In Siberia, people make hundreds of small meat dumplings called "pelmeni" and store them in the frozen ground in winter.

● Russia produces its own sparkling wine, which is traditionally served on birthdays, weddings, and holidays.

fourth largest producer of wheat. Its 1993 production of 46.8 million tons was less than half the total 115.5 million tons of the world's largest producer that year, China.

However, some parts of south European Russia and the areas near Vladivostok in the Far East have warm summers and good soil. Thus salad vegetables, such as tomatoes and peppers, can be grown, as well as fruits, such as plums and watermelons. In the Russian Far East, soybeans are grown. Russians eat cereals that are rarely consumed in the United States. In particular, buckwheat is a popular choice. It is eaten with meat, usually pork or pork sausages, or is made into a porridge, or a soft, thick food.

The poorer soils of north European Russia are suited to the production of vegetables such as cabbages and beets. These two vegetables form the basis of the

▶ *Russian workers and their families normally eat three hot meals a day. This family's supper consists of "zakuski," or appetizers, followed by chicken and a Russian favorite – buckwheat porridge.*

famous Russian soups that include meat and other vegetables and are almost a meal in themselves. They are usually eaten at lunchtime. Cabbage soup is known as SHCHI and beet soup is called BORSCHT. Sour cream is added when the soup is served, and normally black rye bread accompanies the dish.

To preserve food for the long winter, Russians traditionally use methods such as pickling and salting. Pickled cucumbers and mushrooms are favorites, as are salted herrings, which may be served as a first course along with salad and salami.

Russian breakfast can come in several forms. It may consist of a hot cereal made with oatmeal or buckwheat, an omelette or fried eggs, or Russian pancakes, known as BLINIS. Lunch can be eaten any time from noon to 4 P.M., but it is normally served around 1 P.M. to 2:30 P.M. It often begins with a fish or meat salad, followed by soup, then meat and potatoes, dessert, and coffee. Or, the main course might be fried

▲ *These combine harvesters are working together to bring in the wheat on the fertile Russian steppes. This is one of the largest collective farms in European Russia, covering 74,100 acres (30,000 ha).*

◄ *A rich harvest of red and yellow peppers is collected every year in the Stavropol region of southern Russia. Farmers also grow wheat, corn, sunflowers (for oil), and various fruits here. It is one of the country's most fertile areas.*

or baked fish, chosen from a great variety of sea or river fish. Russia's most famous fish is the sturgeon that lives in the Caspian Sea. It can weigh as much as 1 ton and live for up to 75 years. The eggs, or roe, of the female sturgeon are canned as caviar, an expensive delicacy that is exported all over the world. Caviar from Russia is considered very special.

Because of the size of the country, Russian farms can be very large – up to 247,000 acres (100,000 ha). These were established by the former Soviet regime. All the farmworkers jointly owned the crops and animals, so they were called "collective" farms. Animal collective farms specialize in rearing cattle, pigs, sheep, or chickens. In the north of European Russia and Siberia, there are reindeer collective farms. Reindeer farming requires special skills. Since the animals naturally migrate in search of food, the farmers have to move with their reindeer. On the large cereal-producing farms of the steppes, teams of combine harvesters are needed to bring in the harvest.

There are also private farms in Russia – 280,000 of them in January 1996 – but these farmers own only 2 percent of the country's total agricultural land. More than half of private farmers own 50 acres (20 ha) or less of land.

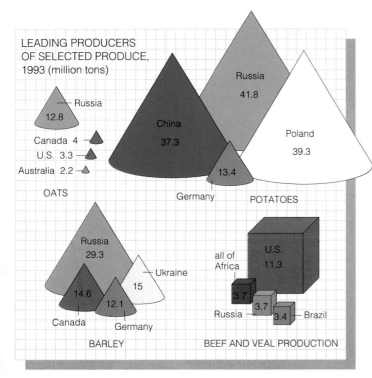

LEADING PRODUCERS OF SELECTED PRODUCE, 1993 (million tons)

OATS
Russia 12.8
Canada 4
U.S. 3.3
Australia 2.2

POTATOES
Russia 41.8
China 37.3
Poland 39.3
Germany 13.4

BARLEY
Russia 29.3
Canada 14.6
Germany 12.1
Ukraine 15

BEEF AND VEAL PRODUCTION
U.S. 11.3
all of Africa 3.7
Russia 3.7
Brazil 3.4

TRADE AND INDUSTRY

In 1994, industry employed 28 percent of Russia's working population. This figure has declined from a total of 30 percent in 1990. Since Russian independence after the fall of the Soviet Union in 1991, there have been dramatic changes in the structure of Russian industry. The country has abundant natural resources, including oil, natural gas, and coal, so mineral products form a significant part of its exports.

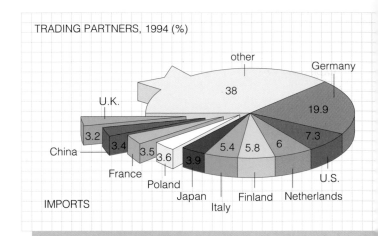

TRADING PARTNERS, 1994 (%)

other 38
Germany 19.9
U.S. 7.3
Netherlands 6
Finland 5.8
Italy 5.4
Japan 3.9
Poland 3.6
France 3.5
China 3.4
U.K. 3.2

IMPORTS

◀ *An assembly line of trucks in Naberezhniye Chelny, Tatarstan Republic. The "Kamaz" trucks built here are among the best-known in Russia.*

▶ *Magnitogorsk's metalworks is the largest in Russia. It produced 17.5 million tons of steel in 1993.*

MANUFACTURING

The proportion of people employed in manufacturing fell from 83% of the total workforce in 1990 to 53% in 1994. At the same time the proportion of those working in the private sector grew from 12.5% to 33%. This reflects the scale of recent privatization. The private sector of the economy now produces 25% of Russia's wealth.

The iron and steel industry remains important. Russia is the world's third largest

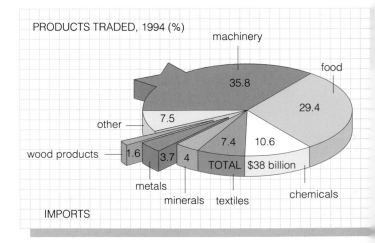

PRODUCTS TRADED, 1994 (%)

machinery 35.8
food 29.4
chemicals 10.6
textiles 7.4
minerals 4
metals 3.7
wood products 1.6
other 7.5

TOTAL $38 billion

IMPORTS

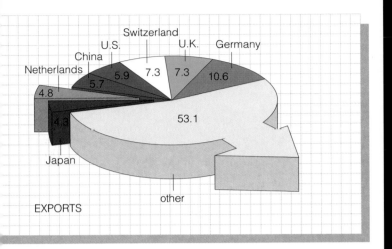

Switzerland
U.S.
China
Netherlands
U.K.
Germany

4.8
4.3
5.7
5.9
7.3
7.3
10.6

53.1

Japan

other

EXPORTS

producer of pig iron and the fourth most important producer of steel. Major industrial centers are located around Moscow in the European part of the country, in the Ural industrial region, and in south Siberia. Within south Siberia, industry is found in an area known as the Kuznetsk Basin or Kuzbass, around the city of Novokuznetsk.

Car and truck manufacturing is located in Moscow and at Tol'yatti on the Volga River. In 1993, Russia produced 956,000 private cars, 526,000 motorcycles, and 1.7 million electrically powered trolleybuses. Some 89,000 tractors were manufactured, along with 33,000 combine harvesters.

FOREIGN TRADE

In 1994, Russian exports were worth almost twice the cost of the country's imports, with exports valued at U.S.$ 64 billion, compared with U.S.$ 38 billion in imports.

Russia's trade is conducted mainly with European countries, with Germany in the primary position for both imports and exports. Other important partners are China and Japan. Household goods, such as

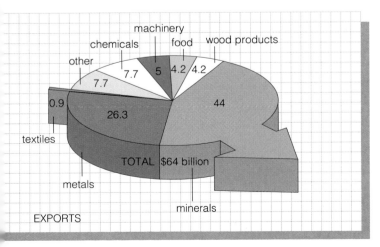

machinery
chemicals
food
wood products
other

7.7
7.7
5
4.2
4.2

0.9
26.3
44

textiles

TOTAL $64 billion

metals

minerals

EXPORTS

kitchen utensils from China and Japan, are found in Russian stores. The U.S. also trades with Russia, and Russia imports more from the U.S. than it exports. Machinery, machine parts, and food form the main basis of Russian imports, while minerals and metals are the basis of its exports. In 1994, Russia exported 101,200 tons of crude oil and 42,900 tons of refined oil and oil products. Natural gas exports totaled 143 billion cubic yards (109 billion m³), making Russia the world's leading exporter of natural gas.

TRAVEL AND TOURISM

There have been recent changes in the amount of travel to and from Russia. The number of foreign visitors fell from 5.4 million in 1993 to 3.3 million in 1994. The proportion of those who were tourists remained the same, at 28% each year. However, in 1995 the number of visitors

▲ **The Labyrinth Company is jointly owned by Russian, British, and Austrian firms and has several trading halls in Moscow. It is one of many joint ventures in Russia today.**

rose to 5.2 million. Russia expects a tourist boom by the year 2000, with a projected 15 million people visiting the country annually. Meanwhile, the number of Russians traveling abroad increased from 8.5 million in 1993 to 9.1 million in 1994. At that time the proportion of those who were tourists rose from 19% to 28%.

The neighboring states of Estonia and Lithuania were the top two destinations for Russians traveling abroad in 1994. Next came Turkey, which is popular for shopping trips. Nearly three times as many Russians visited the U.S. compared with the number of Americans who traveled to Russia.

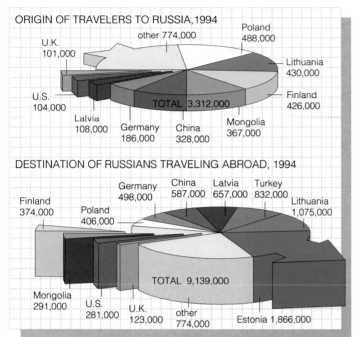

ORIGIN OF TRAVELERS TO RUSSIA, 1994

- other 774,000
- Poland 488,000
- U.K. 101,000
- Lithuania 430,000
- Finland 426,000
- U.S. 104,000
- TOTAL 3,312,000
- Latvia 108,000
- Germany 186,000
- China 328,000
- Mongolia 367,000

DESTINATION OF RUSSIANS TRAVELING ABROAD, 1994

- Germany 498,000
- China 587,000
- Latvia 657,000
- Turkey 832,000
- Finland 374,000
- Poland 406,000
- Lithuania 1,075,000
- TOTAL 9,139,000
- Mongolia 291,000
- U.S. 281,000
- U.K. 123,000
- other 774,000
- Estonia 1,866,000

THE RETAIL SECTOR

Since 1992, there has been a great increase in the variety and choice of consumer goods that are available in large Russian cities. More than 250 supermarkets have opened in Moscow. Western brands of toothpaste and chocolate bars are among the most popular imported items.

▼ *GUM, one of Russia's oldest department stores, is in Moscow. Following renewal in 1991, it stocks many foreign products.*

Transportation is a major problem in Russia, because of the sheer size of the country and the diversity of its landscape.

Russia has the longest railroad in the world, covering 5,786 miles (9,332 km) between Moscow and Vladivostok, running across East Europe and Siberia. It is known as the Trans-Siberian Railroad. Construction work on the line began more than a century ago, in 1892. It takes six days to complete the journey, and trains can sometimes be as much as 24 hours late.

The second Siberian railroad, built between 1974 and 1985, is known as the Baykal–Amur Mainline, or BAM. It takes part of its name from the famous Siberian Lake Baykal. BAM is 1,950 miles (3,145 km) long, of which more than 1,240 miles (2,000 km) are laid on permafrost. In the spring, when the ice from the permafrost melts, there can be major problems. Ice buildups bend and twist the tracks and make for expensive repairs.

The road network is concentrated in European Russia and extends to eastern Siberia. Most of these roads were built between 1928 and 1950. There is no continuous road across the eastern parts of the country, although there is a separate route in the Far East called the Aldan Highway. A highway between St. Petersburg and Nizhniy Novgorod, via Moscow, is currently being built and is due to open in 1998.

In January 1995, there were 12.4 million private cars in Russia — compared with 143 million in the U.S., whose population is only twice as large. The most popular model is the Lada, while the most popular imported model is the Volvo, from Sweden.

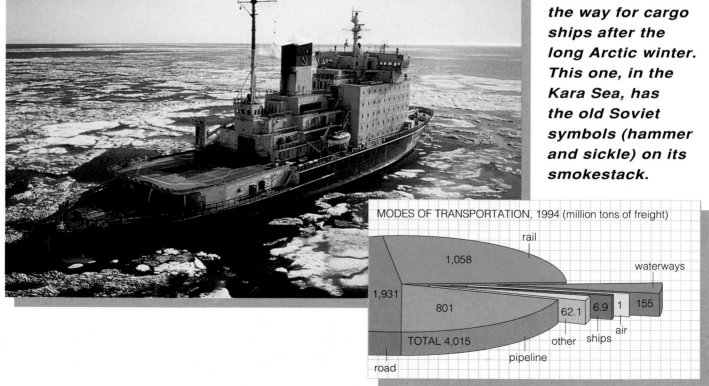

◄ *Russia's icebreakers clear the way for cargo ships after the long Arctic winter. This one, in the Kara Sea, has the old Soviet symbols (hammer and sickle) on its smokestack.*

MODES OF TRANSPORTATION, 1994 (million tons of freight)

rail 1,058

waterways 155

1,931

801

62.1 6.9 1

TOTAL 4,015

other ships air

road pipeline

KEY FACTS

● In 1994, Russia had 460,660 miles (743,000 km) of paved roads, compared with 3.87 million miles (6.24 million km) in the U.S.
● There are 103,400 miles (94,000 km) of waterways and 53,940 miles (87,000 km) of rail track.
● People pay a flat fare to travel any distance on the Moscow or St. Petersburg metros.
● As of January 1996, there were also metro, or subway, systems in 4 other Russian cities.
● Public transportation is free for senior citizens.
● Russia has 110 major airports, and there are also more than 120 airstrips in the north and Siberia.
● Russia has 41 major seaports.
● Car imports totaled 182,461 in 1993, but this fell to 60,653 in 1994.
● Buying a car in Russia means paying the full price of the car at the time of purchase. No credit system is available.

▲ *Helicopters are the only reliable form of transportation during the Arctic winter in remote settlements such as here, on the Chukotka Peninsula in the Far East.*

▼ *The Moskva River is used by commercial shipping, such as these barges, along most of its course.*

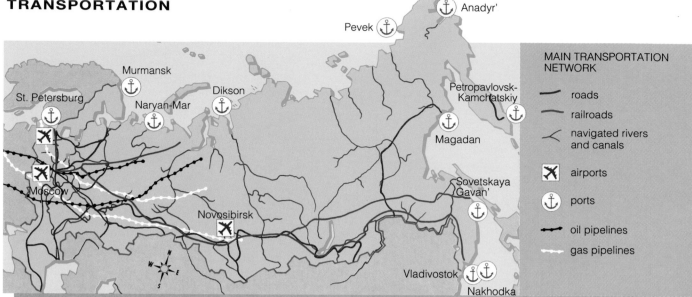

MAIN TRANSPORTATION NETWORK

- —— roads
- —— railroads
- ⟨ navigated rivers and canals
- ✈ airports
- ⚓ ports
- ●–●–● oil pipelines
- ○–○–○ gas pipelines

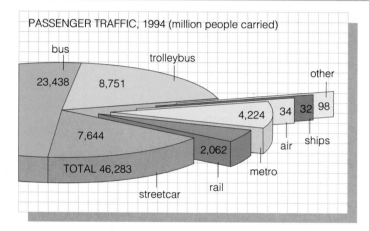

PASSENGER TRAFFIC, 1994 (million people carried)

bus — 23,438
trolleybus — 8,751
streetcar — 7,644
rail — 2,062
metro — 4,224
air — 34
ships — 32
other — 98

TOTAL 46,283

▶ *The Trans-Siberian Railroad crosses many of Russia's diverse landscapes, including some of the least populated regions of Siberia.*

Pipelines form another important part of the transportation network. They are used to transport oil and natural gas.

In the northern parts of Russia, especially Siberia, air transportation is often the only means of moving people and goods. Helicopters are used in the remote areas, since they do not require a runway and can land on snow and ice without difficulty. The Russian national airline is called Aeroflot. Since 1990 it has been divided into separate companies, and by 1995 there were more than 50 of these.

The airlines now seen at European airports, along with Aeroflot, are usually Russian International Airlines and Transaero.

For many years the Russians have attempted to develop an ocean route along the Arctic coast. This is usually known as the Northern Sea route. In spite of the use of modern icebreakers, the harsh environment here still causes problems. For example, in October 1983 the eastern part of the Arctic Ocean froze solid and trapped seven ships for nearly six months.

THE ENVIRONMENT

◀ *The oil industry has created many environmental problems. This oil leak at Usinsk in 1994 took months to clean up.*

▼ *Once common in European Russia, brown bears are now found chiefly in Siberia and the Far East. In 1994, there were 125,800 of them.*

R ussia's various regions have different environmental problems and advantages.

European Russia has a very long history of economic development. As a result, more than half of its old forests have been cut down over the last three centuries, and animal life has been depleted. Recent attempts to remedy this have included reintroducing certain species, such as European bisons, that are now protected.

Central regions, including Moscow, have serious problems with water and air pollution. In the southern part of European Russia, huge dams built on the Volga River have blocked the way to the traditional spawning grounds of the precious sturgeon.

Unique European antelopes called "saigas" still graze on the steppes of Kalmykia near the Caspian Sea, as they have since ancient times. But the raising of too many sheep and cattle has destroyed the fragile sandy soils and created a desert here.

Since Siberia and the Far East are more sparsely populated, there are fewer overall

NATURE PRESERVES AND NATIONAL PARKS

- nature preserves less than 247,000 acres (100,000 ha)
- nature preserves greater than 247,000 acres (100,000 ha)
- □ national parks

▶ **The Amur, or Ussurian tiger, lives in the forests of the southern Far East. Although it is a protected species, some animals can be seen in zoos across the world. Recently, its numbers have declined because of poaching.**

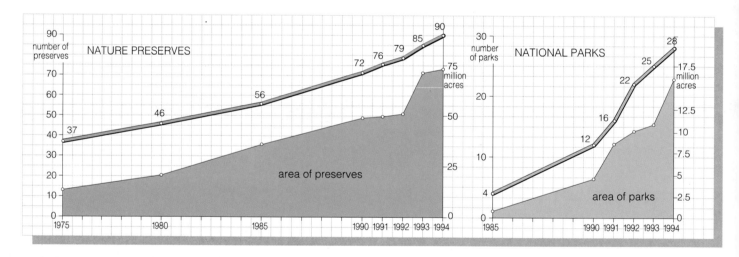

NATURE PRESERVES

number of preserves: 90, 85, 79, 76, 72, 56, 46, 37

area of preserves

1975 1980 1985 1990 1991 1992 1993 1994

NATIONAL PARKS

number of parks: 28, 25, 22, 16, 12, 4

area of parks

1985 1990 1991 1992 1993 1994

problems. But in some places, the oil, natural gas, and coal industries have had an adverse impact. Tundra landscapes are very fragile, as it takes 70 years for reindeer moss to grow to its normal height of just a few inches. Over the last 30 years, nearly 15 million acres (6 million ha) of reindeer pasture have been destroyed by the effects of the oil and gas industries.

There are more than 1,400 species of

plant and animal life in Lake Baykal. More than half are unique, including the scaleless deepwater Golomyanka fish and the world's only freshwater seal. But industry poses threats here, too. A pulp and paper plant at Baykalsk has been polluting the lake for more than 30 years, despite the opposition of environmentalists.

Siberian forests have always been rich in furbearing animals such as sable and

ermine. These have been used to decorate royal robes. There are also mink, polecats, polar and silver foxes, and squirrels here. Large mammals, such as elk, live in the taiga, too, and there is one elk-raising farm in European Russia.

In the south of the Far East, there are unique contrasting landscapes known as "Ussurian taiga" where northern and southern species of trees grow together, including the Siberian larch and Mongolian oak. Both brown and black bears live here, along with snow leopards and Amur tigers. The Japanese thrush is one of many bird species in this area.

Despite its problems, Russia has one of the world's best systems of protected areas. About 15 percent of its territory, mainly in Siberia, is untouched by humans. Throughout the country there are preserves, where people are only allowed to visit for purposes of study. National parks are also popular with tourists.

KEY FACTS

● Russian forests cover 1,904.7 million acres (771.1 million ha), or 45% of the total territory.
● In 1994, more than one million acres (500,000 ha) of forests were destroyed in 20,000 fires.
● Transportation is responsible for two-thirds of air pollution in Moscow. During rush hours, emissions are 3 times greater than the maximum permitted level.
● Since 1978, the level of the Caspian Sea has risen by more than 6.5 feet (2 m), bringing the threat of flooding.
● More than 3,000 square miles (8,000 sq km) of Russian land are still contaminated by radiation, 10 years after the accident at Chernobyl (Ukraine) in 1986.

◀ *Moscow's Cathedral of Christ the Savior is a symbol of recent changes. After the 1917 Revolution, it was demolished and replaced by a swimming pool. Work on its reconstruction began in January 1995, and it was completed in just 12 months – four years ahead of schedule.*

▶ *The Arbat is a fashionable area in central Moscow, which has always been popular with writers and artists. It now has a McDonald's Restaurant as well.*

Despite many environmental and economic problems, Russia's economy is growing and inflation has slowed down. With a wealth of natural resources and a well-educated labor force, Russia has great potential.

Emphasis on the development of mineral-rich regions in Siberia and the Far East is expected to continue. Russians are using existing railroads and roads, while building new ones jointly with Western companies. Exchange of technologies will involve sharing the unique approach to eye surgery developed by Russian doctors and the flow

KEY FACTS

● About 3–5% of the population have an annual income of more than U.S.$ 120,000. They are known as "New Russians."

● In 1997, Moscow celebrates its 850th anniversary. Russia's first underground shopping complex will open in the city.

● By the middle of the 21st century, about 75% of all passenger air travel will be routed across Russia and the North Pole.

● Russia's agricultural system has been transformed. The country is likely to become an exporter of cereals by the year 2005.

of Western technologies into Russia. Current joint efforts include research into how to help children affected by the Chernobyl disaster.

An agreement signed with Belarus, Kazakhstan, and Kyrgyzstan in 1996 shows that Russia is creating closer links with the former Soviet republics. It is also more open to the world economy, and its share of exports to Western Europe and North America is ready to grow.

Since Russia has become less militarized, strategic regions in the Arctic areas that have been closed to international air traffic will be opened up. This will dramatically change global travel routes, saving time by linking North America with Eurasia by way of the North Pole.

There is a long-term plan to build a channel under the 50-mile (80-km) Bering Strait that divides Eurasia and North America and to construct a railroad through it. This will make the division of the world into East and West meaningless. Some hope to build a transcontinental highway from Western Europe via Russia into North America.

Since 1991, more Russians have been able to travel to foreign countries, and more people from abroad have visited Russia. This trend continues to open up the country to new ideas and influences, particularly among the younger generation.

▶ *In 1991, a millionaires' club was formed in Moscow. Today there are many billionaires in the country, too. Ilya Mitkov, pictured here, is one of the youngest of them.*

FURTHER INFORMATION

- AEROFLOT (AIRLINES)
235 W. 48th Street
New York, NY 10036
- EMBASSY OF THE RUSSIAN FEDERATION
1706 18th Street, NW
Washington, DC 20009
- RUSSIAN INFORMATION SERVICES
89 Main Street, Suite 2
Montpelier, VT 05602 *(Catalogs only)*
- RUSSIAN TOURIST INFORMATION
800 Third Avenue, New York, NY 10022

BOOKS ABOUT RUSSIA

Buettner, Dan. *Sovietrek: A Journey by Bicycle Across Russia.* Lerner Group, 1994
Cumming, David. *Russia.* Thomson Learning, 1994
Gillies, John. *The New Russia.* Silver Burdett Press, 1994
Kotlyarskaya, Elena. *Women in Society: Russia.* Marshall Cavendish, 1994
Torchinsky, Oleg. *Russia.* (Cultures of the World Series.) Marshall Cavendish, 1994

GLOSSARY

BLINI
A Russian pancake made with wheat flour and served with minced meat or jam.

BORSCHT
Pronounced "borshuss." Russian beet soup with meat, potato, carrot, onion, and cabbage, served with sour cream.

CHERNOZEM
An extremely fertile, black-colored soil, with a rich organic top layer that may be more than 3 feet (1 m) deep.

COMMUNISM
An economic and political system in which private ownership is abolished and all industry is controlled by the state. The Soviet Union was a Communist state until 1991.

PATRIARCH
Head of the Russian Orthodox Church and the spiritual leader of Russian Christians.

PERMAFROST
A layer of permanently frozen earth in Russia's north and across most of Siberia. It has remained frozen since the end of the last Ice Age and can be 3–2,625 feet (1–800 m) thick.

PRIVATIZATION
The process of selling state-owned factories and stores to private individuals or groups of shareholders. In Russia, this process started in 1992 and was virtually complete by December 1995.

SHCHI
Pronounced "sheee." A thick cabbage soup with meat, onion, garlic, potato, and carrot, served with sour cream.

STEPPE
A landscape of tall grasses, resistant to drought and frost, with a few shrubs along river valleys. The steppes form the major wheat-growing areas of Russia.

TAIGA
The area of coniferous forest that stretches from the western border of Russia across Siberia and the Far East. It forms the largest forest in the world.

TSAR
The title of the Russian monarchs who ruled from 1547 to 1917.

TUNDRA
The treeless landscape north of the taiga. It consists of mosses, marsh plants, and shrubs.

INDEX

A

age structure 21
agriculture 28–31, 33, 42
air transportation 37, 38, 42, 43
Alexei II, Patriarch 24
animals 39, 40–41
Arctic Russia 10, 14, 20, 24, 29, 37, 38, 43
army 27
Asiatic Russia 8, 11, 18, 22

B

Baltic Sea 8, 10
Barnaul 15
Baykal, Lake 11, 12, 36, 40
Baykalsk 40
Belarus 43
Belorussians 18
Bering Strait 43
Black Sea 10, 13, 14, 15
blinis 30
borscht 30
Buddhism 22

C

cars 33, 36–37
Caspian Sea 10, 15, 31, 39, 41
Cathedral of Christ the Savior, Moscow 42
Catholicism 22
Caucasus 10
Chechnya Republic 27
Chernobyl 9, 41, 43
chernozem 10
Chukotka Peninsula 37
cities 9, 19, 20
climate 13–15
clothes 20
coal mining 16
Communism 26, 27

D

dachas 22, 25
deserts 10
diamonds 16

E

economy 9
education 13, 22–23, 25
Elbrus, Mount 9
Elizabeth II, Queen of England 26
Entsi 18
environment 9, 39–41
Estonia 34
European Russia 8, 10, 11, 15, 16, 18, 22, 29, 31, 33, 36, 39, 41

F

families 8, 21, 29
Far East, Russian 10, 11–12, 13, 15, 16, 17, 18–20, 21, 24, 29, 36, 37, 39–40, 41, 42
farming 28–31, 33, 42
festivals 22, 25
flags 26
food 20, 21, 22, 28–31
forests 10, 12, 16, 17, 39, 40–41

G

gold 17
government 26–27
GUM (department store) 35

H

health care 23, 24, 42
helicopters 37, 38
history 8–9
housing 8, 19, 20, 22, 25

I

industry 9, 32–33, 40
Irkutsk 28
iron and steel industry 32–33
Irtysh River 12
Islam 9, 22

J

Jews 22
Judaism 22

K

Kalmykia 10, 39
Kara Sea 36
Kazakhstan 43
Klyuchevskaya Sopka 11
Kremlin 27
Kursk 16
Kuznetsk Basin 33
Kyrgyzstan 43

L

Labyrinth Company 34
landscape 10–12, 41
legal system 27
Lena River 9, 12
life expectancy 9, 21
Lithuania 34
Luzhkov, Yuri 26

M

Magnitogorsk 32
manufacturing 32–33
metro systems 23, 37

millionaires' club 43
minerals 16, 17, 32, 34
Mirniy diamond mines 16
monasteries 9
Moscow 9, 13, 15, 17, 20, 23, 24, 27, 29, 33, 35, 36, 37, 39, 41, 42, 43
Moskva River 37
mountains 10–12

N

Naberezhniye Chelny 32
Narodnaya, Mount 11
national parks 40, 41
nationalities 18–20
natural gas 11, 16, 17, 38, 40
natural resources 9, 16–17, 32, 42
nature preserves 40, 41
Nentsy 18, 20
Neva River 15
nickel 16
Nizhniy Novgorod 12, 36
Novokuznetsk 33
Novosibirsk 9

O

oil industry 11, 16, 17, 38, 39, 40
Oka River 12
Oroki 18

P

Pacific Ocean 8, 15
Patriarch 24
Pechora National Park 11
permafrost 9, 12, 16, 17, 36
Peter and Paul Island 15
pipelines 38
police 26, 27
pollution 17, 39, 41
population 9, 18–21
President 26, 27
privatization 9, 32
Protestants 22

R

railroads 36, 37, 38, 42, 43
religions 9, 22, 23, 24
rivers 12
roads 8, 36, 37, 42, 43
Russian Orthodox Church 9, 22, 24, 25
Russian Revolution 8

S

St. Petersburg 9, 15, 36, 37
Sakha Republic 16
samovars 23

schools 13, 22–23, 25
Sea of Japan 15
shchi 30
ships 14, 36, 37, 38
Siberia 8, 10, 11–12, 13, 14, 15, 16, 17, 18–20, 21, 24, 28, 29, 31, 33, 36, 38, 39–41, 42
Slavs 18
Sochi 15
soldiers 27
Soviet Union 8–9, 22, 32, 36, 43
sports 24–25
Stavropol 30
steppes 10, 15, 30, 31
stores 35, 42

T

taiga 10, 11, 12, 17, 41
timber 16, 17
Tol'yatti 33
tourism 34–35
trade 32–35
transportation 36–38, 41
travel 34–35, 43
Trinity and St. Sergius monastery 9
Tsars 8, 26
tundra 10, 40
Turkey 34

U

Ukraine 9, 41
Ukrainians 18
unemployment 33
United Nations 9
Ural Mountains 10–11, 16, 33
Usinsk 39
USSR *see* Soviet Union

V

vacations 14, 22, 25
Verkhoyansk 13
Vladivostok 14, 15, 21, 29, 36
volcanoes 11
Volga River 11, 12, 33, 39

W

weather 13–15

Y

Yakuts 18, 20
Yakutsk 15
Yamal Peninsula 17
Yeltsin, Boris 26, 27
Yenisey River 12

© Macdonald
Young Books 1996

ARCTIC
OCEAN

75°
60°
45°
30°
15°
0°
15°
30°
45°

75° 60° 45° 30° 15° 0° 15° 30° 45° 60° 75° 90° 105° 120° 135° 150° 165° 180° 165° 150° 135° 120° 105° 90° 75°

NORWAY

DEN.

SWEDEN

FINLAND

BARENTS
SEA

KARA
SEA

KARELIA

YAMAL PENINSULA

BALTIC SEA

ESTONIA

St. Petersburg

Arkhangel'sk

LATVIA

POLAND

LITHUANIA

KALININGRAD
OBLAST

Usinsk

KOMI

BELARUS

MOSCOW

RUSSIAN

MOLDOVA

Nizhniy Novgorod

MARI

Kursk

UDMURTIA

UKRAINE

MORDOVIA

TATARSTAN

Naberezhniye Chelny

Yekaterinburg

CHUVASHIA

Tol'yatti

BASHKORTOSTAN

Chelyabinsk

Samara

BLACK
SEA

Volgograd

KARACHAEVO-
CHERKESSIA

Magnitogorsk

Omsk

Novosibirsk

ADYGEYA

KALMYKIA

Stavropol
CHECHNYA

Novokuznets

KABARDINO-
BALKARIA

NORTH
OSSETIA

INGUSHETIYA

DAGESTAN

GORN
ALTA

GEORGIA

KAZAKHSTAN

ARMENIA

AZERBAIJAN

CASPIAN SEA

TURKEY

IRAN

0   500 miles

0   1,000 km

UZBEKISTAN

TURKMENISTAN

KYRGYZSTAN